GREAT GERMAN CARS

Above: Opel 'Doktorwagen' of 1909.
Front endpaper: The Mercedes-Benz C111.

Mercedes-Benz, 1936; elegance and performance. Its eight cylinder unit developed 160 hp with supercharger.

GALLERY BOOKS

An Imprint of W. H. Smith Publishers Inc.

112 Madison Avenue

New York City 10016

GREAT GERMAN CARS

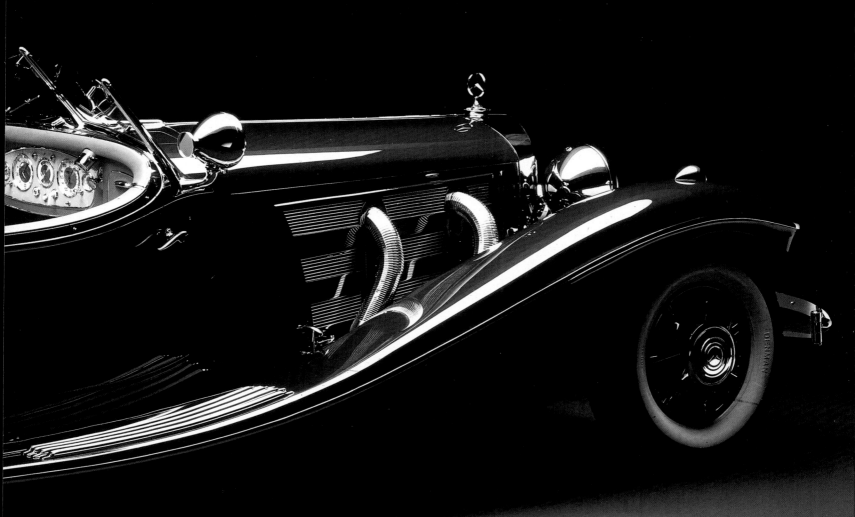

PETER ROBERTS

This book was devised and produced by
Multimedia Publications (UK) Ltd.

Editor: Jeff Groman
Design: Brian Harris
Production: Arnon Orbach

ISBN 0 8317 3988 6

First published in the United States of America by
Gallery Books, an imprint of W.H. Smith Publishers
Inc., 112 Madison Avenue, New York, NY 10016.
Originated by D.S. Colour International Ltd, London

CONTENTS:

Below: Porsche 944.

INTRODUCTION

It is New Year's Eve. The place, the shed in the back yard of the Benz family home in Mannheim. The time 11.55 pm.

Karl Benz has been working on small gasoline engines for years and is almost broke. His latest, bolted to the bench in the shed, obstinately refuses to start. The 35-year-old engineer and his pretty young wife Bertha are not looking forward to the coming year, 1880. This is what Karl Benz wrote about that winter's evening:

> After supper my wife said: 'Let's go over to the shed and try once more. Something tells me to go and will not let me be.' So there we were back again, standing in front of the engine as if it were a great mystery, impossible to solve. My heart was pounding. I turned the crank. The engine started to go put-put, and the music of the future sounded out with regular rhythm . . . like no magic flute in the world ever had. The longer it played the more sorrow and anxiety slipped away from my heart . . . Suddenly the bells began to ring — New Year's Eve Bells. We felt that they were not only ringing in a new year, but a new era.

Prophetic words from a penniless German engineer, words that were to be confirmed the very next year when Benz trundled out his first automobile, the little three-wheeler 'motor-wagen' that was to be the ancestor of them all.

The birth of the first great German marque, and that of Gottlieb Daimler, Benz's contemporary down the road at Cannstatt, set the standard for road transport for the world for many years, and though during the first half of the twentieth century Germany was buffeted by the storms of war, of politics and revolution — and drained by the madness of runaway inflation — the country's automotive industry has returned to high-quality work and high-production figure, sometimes, literally, from the debris and ashes of its former success.

Today there are just six major organizations: Volkswagen, Audi, BMW, Daimler-Benz, Opel and Porsche, but through the pioneering years, the years of development, setback and achievement, there have been many more. Those we briefly meet in this book had several things in common. Engineering quality, that little more than the next manufacturers, that slight edge on the competition from other countries, was perhaps the outstanding feature of a large proportion of them. Early examples may have

Opposite above: World leader in the front-engined GT class the Porsche 928S is a high-performance car for the skilled driver. Opposite left: The 150H Mercedes-Benz (H is for 'Hinter' or rear-engined) housed just 55 hp under its hood behind the driver. It was built in the 'economy' thirties. Above: the Audi Quattro range brings the German company into the four-wheel drive lead. Left: A BMW 328, in its homeland. Since the days of its first fourwheel product BMW had been known for engineering quality.

been lumbering heavies or lightweight buzzboxes but a single strong thread can be seen woven into the fabric of German industry — a dedication to engineering competence. And when disaster struck, as it so often did then, particularly in the bankrupt 1920s when German finances went crazy, they formed life-saver groups to keep afloat, and to hold minimum quality.

Germany in the thirties, at first slow to recover from the US-sparked depression, had by the middle of the decade produced cars – particularly sports cars – that were streets ahead of the world in performance and style. BMW's glorious 328, the Mercedes-Benz 540K, Adler's 2½ liter that could cruise at 80 on the 860 miles of the Third Reich's *autobahnen*, were cars that led their various market categories in Europe. The eager adoption of advanced suspension systems, of front-wheel drive, of synchromesh, overdrive, aerodynamic shapes, all designed with faster, safer travel over longer distances in mind, took German autos way ahead of competitors. War in 1939 halted this flood of engineering excellence, delaying — but not destroying — its flowering for some seven years.

From the rubble of an industry that had been 80 per cent destroyed factories were rebuilt which within a few short years were turning out vehicles which were healthy sellers — and which in the middle 1950s captured the major trophies of motor sport.

The rise of VW to the world's biggest-selling car, the story of BMW from its motorcycle days through the Austin Seven lookalike Dixi to the superb vehicles of the present day, the Audi story of dissent, struggle, survival and merger, the great Mercedes-Benz empire, the wizardry of the company started by Ferdinand Porsche and the steady climb of Opel to Rüsselsheim's reliable machines of today, were all part of the German 'industrial miracle' of the late forties and the fifties.

We have included about twenty other German marques which, although they may have vanished from the showrooms, now still merit a place in history as pioneers, as contributors to technical advance, as innovators, or simply for their stubborn longevity in an industry that saw several thousand makes disappear during its history. Each of these marques here made a contribution: Hanomag's first people's car, Adler's Ace of Trumps of the thirties, DKW's energetic two-cycle unit, Amphicar's plunge into the amphibian world, and so on.

A quote from a Volkswagen history says it all. 'The secret behind Volkswagen's success — *which other manufacturers know but do not care to copy* — is a painstaking integrity of design and manufacture. The customers have noticed...'

Left: Breathed-on BMW. A show-and-go conversion of one of the BMW 3-Series by Alpina. Below: Power and glory, the ultimate in late-thirties luxury and speed was the sleek Mercedes-Benz 540K supercharged sports tourer. This is a 1936 example.

ADLER

Ace of Trumps

Today Adler of Frankfurt is a household name in the competitive word processor market. A long way from the firm's modest start in 1900 but a logical progression from Adler's bid for a slice of the moneymaking bicycle market of the day.

Heinrich Kleyer, Adler's boss, had been in the pedal business since 1886, rival to successful cyclemaker Adam Opel, when the firm landed a small contract to supply parts for the Benz Velo, the first 'series' production car to be built and a car whose wire-spoked wheels were only a sprocket or two away from Adler's bicycle products.

With early offerings of small, relatively cheap cars from Renault, De Dion, Benz, etc, Adler was tempted into the

four-wheeled field. The first Adler, mechanically a Renault lookalike, was a tiny 400 cc job that, with a few improvements had, surprisingly, a claim to fame as one of the first cars to negotiate the dangerous Alpine route from Germany to Italy, then not much more than a stagecoach track.

Bohemian engineer Edmund Rumpler, later to become a pioneer in automotive aerodynamics and a strong influence in motor design, gave Adler's engines a character of their own. One of Rumpler's innovations was a gearbox built in-unit with the motor — a 12 hp twin or a 24 hp four — standard practice in later years. Engine displacements grew rapidly in common with most other marques during the first decade of the twentieth century and Rumpler made some fine L-head side valve units with dual ignition, and cylinders multiplied. A bewildering variety of no less than thirty models were marketed in the late Edwardian days. The Adler four-cylinder 7.4 liter, which caught the eye of Kaiser Wilhelm II, went promptly into his personal motor stable.

In the twenties there was talk of a Chrysler take-over but the Opel purchase by America's General Motors brought a ban on further big overseas deals by the German state. The 1930s saw Adler at their most adventurous with the tremendously successful 1.5 liter Adler Trumpf (Trump) with its all-independent suspension, rack-and-pinion steering and front-drive. At that time there were only two German sports cars that captured the imagination of the rest of the world, the BMW, fast developing into a world-beater, and the streamlined Adler *Rennlimousine,* a geared-up, lightened racing version of the Trumpf Junior, which made a good showing at the Twenty Four Hours of Le Mans in 1937-8.

A super-streamlined wind-tunnel-designed 1939 car was far ahead of its time but too near the start of a war for its full impact to be felt by a world with other things on its mind.

Left: Adler of Frankfurt built its first car in 1900. The model of ten years later shown here is a 3.2 liter sports that proved popular in Europe. Below: Ahead of its time. The Adler Trumpf of 1932 had independent suspension all-round, frontwheel drive and rack-and-pinion steering.

AMPHICAR

A Real Convertible

The French beach shimmered in the heat, and in the distance England's white cliffs seemed almost within call. A small convertible trundled over the sand to the water's edge and stopped. Its driver engaged gear — and with a swirl of propellors the open car chugged away into the sea heading for Britain. The Amphicar was about to create a world record.

Amphibious vehicles were not new, even in 1962 when this pioneering voyage took place. The idea had been successfully tried out around 55 years earlier when a Frenchman had made a canoe-shaped car, powered in the normal way on land, and in the water by propellors, using its front wheels as rudders. In the twenties some students of Wisconsin University had sealed up a Model T Ford and taken it on a local lake. It sank without trace.

During World War II a more serious attempt was made to adapt land vehicles to land/marine use when Volkswagen produced the Schwimmwagen, based on Hitler's Porsche-designed 'Strength Through Joy' car — later to be known as the VW Beetle. The US Army also had several amphibians, the best known of which was the DUKW (more familiarly known as the Duck), a six-wheeler built around a GM truck frame. Some 21,000 Ducks were made and are today cherished collector's items.

The Berlin-made Amphicar was the logical successor to various wartime productions, and by 1962 Hans Trippel, a designer responsible for a number of earlier amphibians, had made his first — and the world's first — civilian personal land/water vehicle.

Powered by a 1147 cc British Triumph engine, the 'vessel' was capable of around 6½ knots, and on land its top speed was 68 mph. Its seaworthiness had been proved in the 1962 Channel crossing, but the roll induced by a flat bottom and a low freeboard of about 18 inches worried nervous passengers a little. Most buyers used it as a leisure car, although some offshore islanders used it for more practical reasons.

Sensibly, it was designed to carry a bilge pump and positive-locking doors, but the rest of the controls and fittings were those of a land vehicle, with the exception of all-round sealing, two small propellors at the stern, and the necessary gearing. Nevertheless, it sank without trace in 1968.

Left: Getting its feet wet here is the Berlin-produced Amphicar, one of the only civilian amphibious vehicles to go into series production. Inset: Driven by a British Triumph power unit the Amphicar could reach around 70 mph on solid ground and some 6½ knots afloat.

Winner with Five Cylinders

Audi had always been a pioneer. Doctor August Horch had founded a company under his own name in 1900 after leaving Benz where he had worked as an engineer, qualifying as one of the first makers of automobiles. He left his own company after designing a big 8 liter white elephant that did not sell, and set up another new company with the name of Audi, the latinized form of his own name.

Dr Horch launched his first Audi from his Zwickau works in 1910 and the following year he drove one successfully in the Alpine Trial, a touring car rally over the daunting mountain passes of Austria. Audi notched two more wins in early Alpine trials, creating a firm reputation for reliability and toughness.

DKW owner J.S. Rasmussen bought the Audi company in 1928. He had been to Detroit, bought up the Rickenbaker machinery lines — the company formed by the famous Captain Eddie Rickenbaker had folded the previous year — and used the American-designed power units in the larger Audi models.

In 1932, Audi and Horch, Wanderer and DKW formed a survival group and called it Auto Union, later to become legendary through the successes of its rear-engined racing cars.

Auto Union was nationalized after World War II. By 1956 Daimler-Benz became the majority shareholder, then Volkswagen obtained control, and by 1965 the name of Audi was seen again on the grill of a 1.7 liter front-wheel-drive sedan with sophisticated features such as disc brakes and independent front suspension. An amalgamation with NSU resulted in the Audi 60 and the 1.8 litre Super 90, a long-life car that can still be seen on the roads of Europe.

Below: By the time this 55 hp two-seater Audi Front was produced the company had joined the Auto Union Group. Right: Audi in the air. One occasion when the Quattro's stabilizing permanent fourwheel drive cannot be used to advantage!

The last years of the sixties saw the Audi in recognizable modern form emerging as the 100 in its various forms, including the coupé, one of the most attractive variants. Its 112 hp front-mounted engine driving the front wheels could lift it from 0 to 60 mph in a brief 9.7 seconds and give it a comfortable cruising speed of 100 mph, ideal for the long straights of Germany's *autobahnen*.

Towards the end of 1972 the Volkswagen influence could be seen grinning through in the smaller Audi 80, a scaled-down version of the 100 with overhead camshaft and four-cylinder motor driving the front wheels in Audi tradition, and greatly improved suspension. VW connections showed too in the even smaller Audi 50, almost indistinguishable from the Polo.

Then in 1976 the five-fingered Audi appeared, and is still current, carving a new pioneering niche for Dr Horch's old company, and when in 1980 the Audi Quattro appeared, developing further the five-cylinder theme with its 2.2 liter pack, Bosch K-Jetronic ignition and full four-wheel drive, the rally branch of motor sport was severely shaken. Here was a contender that could travel comfortably up the north face of an icy alpine pass, could keep up fast cruising speeds over packed snow, handled in streaming rain as though it was a dry day: rally-winning facts which brought Audi a pile of silverware. The machine instils confidence in the driver that no two-wheel drive can give, and today's Audi 200 Turbo Quattro constantly attracts praise from the pundits. The days when the Audi was called the 'poor man's Mercedes' are long gone.

The Audi Quattro's contribution to road stability — its glued-to-the-road fourwheel drive boosts safety at modern speeds in all conditions but shows most in wet when the car may be driven as though the road surface is completely dry. The five-cylinder Quattro's (right and far right) are capable of up to 140 mph in 200 form.
Below: Smartest coupé of the seventies, the 1.8 liter Audi 100S 2+2.

BENZ

Father of the Automobile

Karl Benz, son of a locomotive driver, produced the world's first practical gasoline-driven car at Mannheim in Germany in 1885. The shaky little three-wheeler had tiller steering and a single-cylinder water-cooled engine at the back with a rating of around 1 horsepower. However, it was without a doubt the vehicle (with Gottlieb Daimler's converted carriage launched a few months later) that is the ancestor of the many millions of autos that followed during the next hundred years. This historic car can still be seen at the Deutsches Museum in Munich.

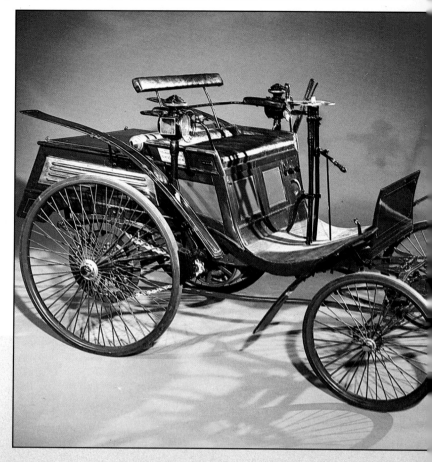

Benz made his first commercially-produced car in 1894, the rear-engined four-wheeled Velo, the first-ever series-manufactured automobile. In 1899 the small Benz company made a total of 572 vehicles which took the firm to the front rank of car manufacturers, most of which were by then French.

The introduction of Daimler's Mercedes in 1901 hit Benz where it hurt. His cars were by then outdated compared with several others in the fast-changing automotive industry, and the Mannheim company was forced to rethink fast, designing front-driven cars, the first of which was the two-cylinder 1903 Parsifal. Karl Benz himself left the company in 1903, joined it again, then moved in 1906 to his son's firm in nearby Ladenburg.

A racing program starting at the turn of the century paid sales dividends for the company as a string of victories kept the Benz name in the forefront of the motor world. By 1908 the Benz Grand Prix car was amongst the most successful of European racers, and its development, the 200 hp streamlined Blitzenbenz, captured the World Land Speed Record in 1911 at 131.72 mph in the hands of Barney Oldfield, the cigar-chewing former showman whose name became synonymous with racing in America.

Benz produced solid, conventional cars during the years leading up to 1914 (including a 22 liter monster which is thought to be the largest private car ever put on the market) ending with the company's first six-cylinder model.

By 1924 the companies of Benz and Daimler, their headquarters only a few miles apart, began to collaborate in their common interest and on 28 June 1926 Benz & Cie amalgamated with the Daimler Motoren Gesellschaft. From these two founders of the motor industry the great Daimler-Benz company, more familiar as Mercedes-Benz, was born.

Left: An 1894 Benz Velo, the world's first series production automobile. Below: Its 1½ liter single-cylinder engine with its slow-turning flywheel. Above: Posters promoted Benz products of the early twenties. Below left: Benz was deeply committed to motor racing by 1908 and entered this 120 hp car in the French Grand Prix of that year.

BMW

From Dixi to M635CSi

Not to be confused with the Dixie from Houston Texas or the Dixie made by the Vincennes Indiana company — or even the Dixie Flyer from the Kentucky Wagon Co — this one was the first-ever car built by Bayerische Motoren Werke (Bavarian Motor Works, or simply BMW). The Dixi was in fact the British Austin Seven built under license. BMW bought the Dixi company and continued building the baby car as their first tentative step into the four-wheel market. Its motorcycles, already well known, provided the cash.

Although internationally known now, the company was not one of the early starters, emerging in 1916 as an amalgam of two other companies, one an airplane manufacturer in Munich with the blue-and-white Bavarian colours in its logo, and the other making marine and aviation engines. The aero engines went into military airplanes and the venture became Bayerische Motoren Werke. But the total marriage did not happen until 1922 when a banker from Vienna bought them both. A wise man as it finally proved, but a buyer who first had to pass through several rough patches.

A 500 cc horizontally opposed twin cylinder engine (normally

Above: BMW's introduction to four wheels; the British-designed Austin Seven first made by the German company in 1928. Below: the 3/15 BMW Dixi is seen in soft-top with very little in its appearance to distinguish it from the then more familiar Austin product. Right: the BMW 328 sports built between 1936-40 and which completely outclassed its opposition. Just 461 were made.

used for stationary work) was put longways into a motor-bike, and after some improvements (at first sketched out on the back of a beer mat) the basic concept never looked back, but it was 1928 before BMW went into the car market with the Eisenach-built Austin Seven Dixi. In 1930 the Dixi, in open two-seater 'roadster' trim, won its class in the famous Monte Carlo Rally after taking the team prize in the Alpine Trial the year before.

The firm really hit the button with its first six-cylinder car, an in-line engine setup which has almost become their trademark. First appearing as an 1175 cc, 30 bhp in 1932, by the next year it was the Model 315 of 1.5 liters with twin carbs and a four-speed gearbox. In its Roadster form this was the first of the line of legendary BMWs. It could reach 75 mph and listed the Alpine Trial among its many trophies.

If any model deserves the description 'classic' it was the beautiful 328 of 1936 of which, sadly, only 462 were made between then and World War II. The 328 calls for special attention on merit, not only because Hitler wanted a sports car to dominate that aspect of racing while Mercedes-Benz and Auto Union were subjugating the Grand Prix circuits of Europe. The 328 possessed

sleeker lines than had ever been seen before, and a performance from its 2-liter (1971 cc) engine that totally outclassed the opposition. In England the Frazer Nash firm (famous in the vintage years for its chain-driven cars) built the 328 for Britain as an FN-BMW.

World War II brought total destruction to the Munich plant and it was 1951 before the company was making cars again. Throughout this decade they were left behind by Mercedes, sliding almost to the edge of bankruptcy in 1959. The first car was the 501, using the 2-liter prewar engine; then came bigger jobs, including BMW's only V8, a car which proved wrong for Germany's poor financial climate, and less than a match for Mercedes' competitive products. In 1954 came the 502, similar in appearance but with the company's 2.6 liter V8 motor turning out 100 bhp, a magical figure that made it the company's best seller of 'real' autos in the fifties with a production of nearly 6,000. The tiny Isetta, produced by BMW to catch the transient bubble car market, reached a production of 162,000 — so the sublime and the ridiculous saved the day for the firm.

BMW's universal appeal blossomed with the launching of the

Top left: A 1938 BMW 328 in action on an English hill-climb circuit some 46 years after the 2-liter car was manufactured. Far left: BMW's first V8 the 2.6 liter 100 mph 502 of 1954. Above top: During the thin years after World War II, BMW looked for ways of surviving and built the 250 cc Isetta bubblecar under licence for a time. Left: a combination decal that looks bizarre today — the marriage of BMW to the little Italian Isetta firm. Above center: Early sports 328 of 1937-39.

2 liter 2002, in effect a move from the exotic to the popular (but not cheap) in 1968. This very roadworthy automobile was intended for the owner who still enjoyed driving, a market that was chosen carefully at the design stage.

When the 525i (fuel injection) came in 1981 it had a top speed of 120 mph from a 150 bhp, 2.5-liter motor; but by 1982 the 635CSi automatic was a 3.5-liter good for 137 mph. This remained the fastest BMW product through to the current M635CSi, developed from the '6' Series 'M' engines by the motor sport department. It captured attention at the 1984 British International Motor Show on introduction to the public, with its 158 mph top speed from its six-cylinder, 24-valve power plant. In recent years BMW road cars have had series identifications 3 to 7 (with 4 excepted). The Series 3 started in the seventies and now Series 7 (728i, 732i, 735i the last two numbers denoting the engine size) is top of the line. Some even say that size-for-size they surpass even Mercedes and Jaguar in the claim for the accolade of the 'ultimate driving machine', as BMW themselves call their product.

Descendant of the 1973 turbo prototype car, the BMW M1, first seen in 1978 was a remarkable publicity exercise. Its midships six cylinder 3450 cc unit, its startling hull-down lines and its top speed of 162 mph made it an unforgettable sight.

Far right: This BMW topline coupé, the 635 CSi, with its modified M1 engine is seen here at Britain's Donington circuit, a prewar racing venue brought back to sporting life during recent years.
Below: A similar model in standard trim is seen at speed. Right: Airborne at Hockenheim.

*Right: A BMW at competition speed.
Below Brabham and BMW engineering are
wedded in this Formula 1 Grand Prix
Brabham-BMW BT53. Here Nelson Piquet,
1983 World Champion, takes his BMW
turbo-engined car through a bend at the
1984 Belgian Grand Prix. Far right: The
elegant M635 CSi at speed.*

BORGWARD

...and the Beautiful Isabella

Wealthy Danish automobile engineer Carl Borgward had bought up a number of firms in Germany during the late 1920s, including the Goliath Werke and Hansa (later Hansa-Lloyd) firms from Bielefeld and Bremen. Hansa was allowed to continue producing under its own name, although under Hitler's later 'Schnell Plan' the range of German cars and its profusion of models was to be cut back in a rationalized program that was to cater for large-scale production of trucks and motorcycles.

The war curtailed Borgward's development and production, mainly centered on Bremen, was turned over to military vehicles. The name Borgward had been seen on only a single model before the war — the 1939 Hansa-built 6 cylinder 1700.

Although the north German city did not escape severe bombing, the dynamic Dane managed to re-enter the civilian automobile field sooner than most. The car first offered to the postwar public in 1949 was a very advanced and stylish Borgward product, a Hansa 1500, with a 52 hp unit giving some 75 mph, a genuine quality product for a time when most carmakers were turning out the same old automobiles as they had offered in 1939.

Borgward dropped the associate name of Hansa soon afterwards, although Lloyd and Goliath 'mini' cars were made in order to climb onto the bubble car bandwagon of the 1950s.

Borgward's most distinguished car, the Isabella, was first seen in 1954 and developed from the postwar range which had grown from the original 1500 cc to 1800 and later to a six-cylinder 2600. Borgward was an early advocate of the diesel engine and these models were sold with that option. The four-cylinder 1½ liter Isabella, a ground-hugger with sleek feminine lines (as all the best cars had then), could attain a surprising top speed of 90 mph. The delightful Isabella — several years ahead of its time aesthetically and mechanically — soon collected a following of enthusiasts who appreciated its 5-seat capacity (although there was also a Touring Sport version with just two places) its all-round independent suspension and its rigid construction. The Isabella also notched high places in racing events in Europe, wins to add to the marque's dozen world-class records set up at France's Montlhéry racetrack in 1950 with a modified 1500.

Borgward had a fine product (the last was a magnificent 2.3 liter) and loyal aficionados, but they just couldn't keep ahead of the creditors. The firm finally closed in 1961.

Left: The delightful unitary-construction Isabella was Borgward's most distinguished product. Introduced in 1954 it was a derivative of the Hansa of the late thirties. Below: The Borgward Isabella was also available in TS (Touring Sport) coupé form with an 1800 cc power unit giving 75 bhp.

DKW

Three Decades a Leader

A latecomer to four-wheel production, DKW (Deutsche Kraftfahrzeug Werke of Berlin) had started life as a maker of motorcycles, along with NSU, BMW, and others, before launching a first car in 1928. Its power unit was, predictably, an ex-bike unit. Its displacement of just over half a liter was indeed small even for those belt-tightening times, but DKW stuck to the two-cycle engine principle right through 38 years of popular production, presenting some highly sophisticated small engines and earning the cars the affectionate nickname of 'Das Kleine Wunder' (The Little Wonder).

The early 1930s saw the first of the DKW Front (front-driven) models, the F1, with a buzzing, crackling little motor of coffee-pot dimensions and high efficiency. It was well made, popular, set the standards for a number of small cars of the day, and was developed into the sleeker 650 cc Meisterklasse which with its contemporaries the Reichsklasse and the 1045 cc Sonderklasse were amongst Germany's most popular small automobiles during the last prewar decade.

Meanwhile DKW had become part of a larger combine when their boss, Jörgen Rasmussen, already the major part-owner of Audi (which purchase also brought Horch and Wanderer into the Rasmussen fold), grouped the names under the four-ring logo of Auto Union, a new conglomerate that could be compared in size with the then recently-formed Daimler-Benz consortium.

In 1950 DKW moved its location to Dusseldorf — it had been in the Soviet zone — and revived the feature that the company had found so successful before the war, the two-cycle power-pack.

Now calling itself DKW-Auto Union, the company manufactured a modern-bodied Meisterklasse, based on the

MONACO

11 ET 13 AVRIL 1936

IMP. MONÉGASQUE . MONTE . CARLO

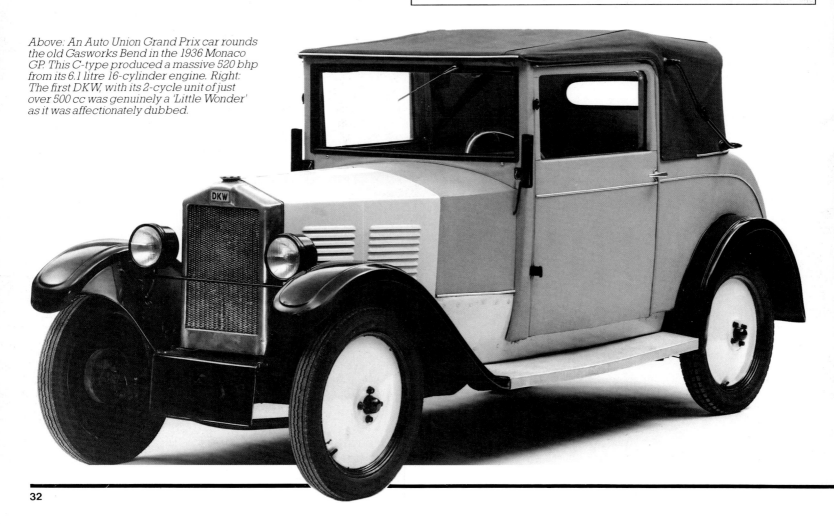

Above: An Auto Union Grand Prix car rounds the old Gasworks Bend in the 1936 Monaco GP. This C-type produced a massive 520 bhp from its 6.1 litre 16-cylinder engine. Right: The first DKW, with its 2-cycle unit of just over 500 cc was genuinely a 'Little Wonder' as it was affectionately dubbed.

prewar car. Then so integrated were the companies under the new Auto Union banner that names were switched and some products from DKW were marketed as Auto Unions (memories of prewar racing success by that marque were still good for sales promotion) and DKWs were also made independently in East Germany as the Trabant.

The DKW-inspired two-cycle engines were highly suitable for a new range of small cars — of which the 34 hp 714 cc Junior was probably the most popular along with the 980 cc Coupé of the early 1960s.

Partnership with Daimler-Benz (better known in other parts of the world as Mercedes-Benz) followed in 1956 and when economic conditions improved and enthusiasm for two-stroke engines waned, the line was eventually dropped in 1966. However, some of the Rasmussen principles of the past are still evident in the present Audi range.

Above: Encouraged by Hitler, Auto Union formed a racing team in 1934 fielding a Porsche-designed rear-engined car. By 1935 the V16 unit had been enlarged from 4.4 to 4.9 liters. Left: This coupé of 1962 was one of the last of DKW's models. Interest in 2-cycle power had waned as economic conditions in Europe improved.

DURKOPP

Sewing Machines, Cars, and Back Again

Although the Bielefeld-made Durkopp may not fall recognizably into the category of great or well-known marque, it merits inclusion here as one of the longest survivors — 28 uninterrupted years — of the early automotive industry in a country that has had more than its share of recessions and disasters.

Durkopp, firmly established in the sewing machinery market, began making automobiles in 1899 with twin-cylinder vehicles built on the 'Systeme Panhard', i.e. front-mounted motor followed by clutch, gearbox and final drive, which although it became the conventional drive layout, was then by no means the standard power-train sequence for a road vehicle.

The Durkopp sales policy was smarter than most. Domestic sales were only part of the business and the company opened a branch in France where they were called Canello-Durkopp, and in Great Britain — where there was pitifully small competition — under the name Watsonia.

Engine sizes had increased to three and six cylinders by 1903 and the company seemed to find its market in stolid touring cars rather than in motor sport, in which so many other marques were struggling to gain supremacy.

A single sporting win in the 1907 Kaiserpreis, however, had set the standard, and the cars were based on the 7.2 liter that took part in that Kaiser-sponsored race, a hugely popular once-only event for touring cars held over the Taunus Mountains near Frankfurt. The touring Durkopp of the day developed 100 hp but needed 13 liters of motor to produce that high figure.

Post-World War I Durkopps sold successfully against the then major marques of Opel, Benz and Mercedes, and several sizes were manufactured from small 8 hp runabouts to a sports car which used an early form of supercharger to obtain some 60 hp.

Durkopp survived Germany's nightmare inflation of the 1920s but stopped making cars in 1927, continuing for just two more years with trucks. However, Durkopp of Bielefeld, a name that never hit the headlines, has survived to the present — when other more famous names have vanished — through the manufacture of scooters, bicycles, and now the full circle: industrial sewing machines and other service equipment.

More signs of Panhard influence than sewing-machine ancestry here in this Durkopp tonneau of 1901. An 1800 cc 8 hp motor with two bucket-sized cylinders powered this smart pioneer auto from Bielefeld Germany.

HANOMAG

The First 'People's Car'

It was so narrow that it could turn corners without a differential, it had a slab-sided body reminiscent of the 1950s, it was propelled by a chain-driven one-cylinder motor that had never grown up — and it sold in large numbers. The time was 1924, the place of manufacture Hanover, and most of the buyers German. It was its ugly squared-off look that earned it the name of *Kommissbrot*,

meaning Army Loaf, which had been more or less the same shape. Its body was the last word in non-aerodynamics and its two side-by-side seats were made only for the slimmer German. A single headlamp gave a fitful light and its overall weight was a flyaway 816 lbs. But it gave almost 16,000 working families a longed-for freedom of travel — a 'People's Car' well before the VW Beetle and the era of mass personal transportation.

Hanomag was not new to the transport business. The company had made locomotives since the last century and trucks since 1905. Known for the durability of its products the firm was unusually successful with its first car, and built the 2/10 hp Army Loaf until 1928 when competition from Dixi, a version of Britain's baby Austin Seven made under license at Eisenach, and the continued high sales record of Opel's larger Laubfrosch (Treefrog), forced Hanomag to produce a larger car.

By the early thirties Hanomag were turning out the Teutonic norm for the period — front-wheel drive cars of a liter and up and called such Wagnerian names as Sturm, Kurier and Garant — the six-pot 2.250 cc Sturm being the flagship — a range little different from the rest of the market although at RM 2700 (about $675) for the Kurier in 1937 the prices were high.

Hanomags scored wins in rallies and hill climbs during the late thirties and by 1939 were offering several models that were aerodynamically well ahead of their time (although front ends tended to look slightly like the Chrysler Airflow from the USA) with unitary construction and a drag coefficient half a generation in advance of the rest. Hanomag pioneered the use of the diesel engine in private cars, the 1910 cc Rekord making its début at the 1936 Berlin Motor Show, and a futuristic aerodynamic Diesel Rekord built for record-breaking doing just that in 1939 when it captured a number of world records for diesel cars.

A spin-off was their popularity in Sweden during World War II where their low compression motors accepted a charcoal adaption, and Hanomag tried to make a comeback with its 'Partner' in 1951 but the vehicle didn't attract customers. So the company returned to making trucks.

A pre-Beetle people's car, The Hanomag 2/10HP, commonly known as the Kommissbrot (Army Loaf) due to its slab-sided shape, offered motoring in its most basic form. Housing a coffee-cup engine of half-a-liter and a spartan body, it nevertheless gave mobility to a large number of people who could never have afforded a more luxurious vehicle. This is a 1926 model.

HORCH

Large and Luxurious

Germany's new road system of the late 1930s demanded a new aerodynamic shape for the increasingly fast-moving cars of the day. Such a car was the Horch autobahn-cruiser built to take full advantage of fast travel, a large V8, 3.8 liter car that rivalled Mercedes in its luxury and style — although its lines look a little clumsy today — a car that was used as a state parade conveyance by many a minor Nazi who didn't quite rate a Mercedes.

Forty years earlier August Horch had broken away from the boredom of his engineering job with Karl Benz at Mannheim where his chief had considered that his horseless carriage with its rear engine and Victorian ironwork was the ultimate in automobile production. Dr Horch had, by 1900, built his own first vehicle, a 5 hp twin cylinder with front-mounted motor, the first German production car with a shaft-driven rear axle. Horch had moved out of his nineteenth-century job into twentieth-century production — and had made a better vehicle than Benz.

Horch moved to a small works at Zwickau in Saxony where a four cylinder model with a displacement of 2.7 liters established Horch as a serious contender in the field. Amongst his early designs was 18/22 hp car that pioneered the clean-lined torpedo style that was to become almost the standard design of the

twenties. Horch had ordered the tall bodies cut down in height to reduce drag — and a new automobile shape was born.

August Horch left his company in 1906 to set up the Audi company, whilst Horch Motorwagenwerke AG continued to build a bewildering number of models under the old name.

The Zwickau firm tended to build big, strong and heavy, aiming at upmarket buyers, and by 1914 the flagship was an enormous 33/80 hp with 8.4 liters under the hood.

Paul Daimler, son of the great Gottlieb, joined Horch in 1923 and applied his considerable talents to a straight-8 with twin overhead camshafts (and later with some very advanced four-wheel air-brakes), followed by the most elegant Horch ever made, the 6 liter V12 90 mph 670, sleek, low and sporting and bearing a coy resemblance to the Mercedes-Benz range. The economics of the time forced Horch to trim its designs, and sizes were reduced sharply in following models. In 1945 Horch (since 1932 a member of Auto Union) found itself on the eastern side of the German border where large luxury automobiles were not at all fashionable. The old factory at Zwickau switched over to small-motored fiber bodied vehicles called Trabants.

Horch, Wanderer, Audi and DKW had formed a survival group in 1932, calling it Auto Union. The four partner marques then carried both their own logo and that of Auto Union itself (left). One of the luxury Horch productions was this 830BL of 1939 (right) sporting a lively 3.8 liter unit giving 92 bhp. Overleaf: A contemporary was the 5 liter 853 seen here in sport cabriolet trim.

MAYBACH

Son of the Mercedes Designer

Germany perhaps more than any other country on either side of the Atlantic has been buffeted by the raw winds of economics. The market in the early 1920s was unpredictable due to runaway inflation, when the necessary cash to buy a meal one day could have bought a car a couple of months earlier, and to the later world depression that forced a radical change in automobile design, quality and size. It was not difficult for the most brilliant of designers, even in a country of the world's finest engineers, to get the wrong car on to the market at the wrong time.

One such was Karl Maybach, son of Wilhelm. Maybach senior had been Daimler's collaborator from the earliest days of the automobile. Some even say that Willi Maybach should share the title of father of the car, and that it was his engineering genius that supported the great Daimler's inventive intellect. It was Maybach

who designed the famous 35 hp Mercedes, the first great twentieth-century step forward in automotive development, and it was he who designed the modern spray carburettor, another automotive landmark.

Maybach senior left Daimler in 1907. Gottlieb his benefactor was dead and old friends had also left. Airship builder Count Ferdinand von Zeppelin needed a new engine — his last had caused him to crash-land his huge hydrogen-filled dirigible. Wilhelm Maybach, an old hand at adapting power to bizarre uses, was called in, but it was son Karl who finally designed the large engines.

How successful Karl was, Londoners discovered a few years later as vast Maybach-engined Zeppelins airships hovered over the British capital showering it with bombs.

In 1919 Karl turned to automobile engines, producing units for various motor-makers, finally deciding to build his own cars. He improved further on his father's ideas bringing a fresh approach to automobile design. He favored a solid box frame, developed a one-movement starter throttle, a planetary gearbox, and his first car, the Maybach W3 of 1921, was also Germany's first car to have four-wheel brakes and a cooling fan that cut out in cold temperatures. The W3 was brilliant, sophisticated, ahead of its time. A little too far ahead at a time when Germany's finances were in deep trouble. However, clothed in coachwork by Spöhn & Glaser, Maybach's specialist bodybuilders, it sold well for a time.

Young Maybach went doggedly on, producing a 7 liter and in

1929 unveiled his big V12 which was followed quickly (in 1932) by the famous Zeppelin automobile, also housing a V12 of 8 liters and a tigerish 200 hp under the long hood. The DS8 Maybach Zeppelin — all 3½ tons of it — was stylish, fast, had eight forward speeds — and an enormous pricetag. The car was a strong contender for the title of the finest automobile ever produced in Germany, although some critics vowed that it should be put in a class of its own and prospective owners should apply for a motor bus license.

During the mid-thirties Maybach produced smaller cars, the DHS and SW series — not that one could place them in any but the first rank. Top-class engineering, speed and comfort were there in plenty and the 6 cylinder units were large enough (the smallest was 3.5 liters, larger than 90 per cent of production cars in Europe at the time) to propel the vehicles in effortless regal silence. The company ceased production in 1941.

Two views of the Maybach SW38 of 1937. In the first rank of cars of its day this was a smaller product from the Friedrichshafen plant, housing just 3.8 liters of potent engineering under the hood. One of the most elegant examples out of Germany in the thirties, Maybachs were designed by the son of the original Mercedes creator.

MERCEDES -BENZ

Founders of an Industry

The regular beat and hiss of machinery could be heard coming from the summer-house at the end of the garden. Outside in the darkness of the Gartenstrasse a posse of Royal Württemberg Police waited impatiently for orders. Gottlieb Daimler answered their knock. 'We have information that you are manufacturing counterfeit currency notes,' said the inspector. Engineer Daimler, who had been living in the German town of Bad Cannstatt for only a short while, asked them in to his ramshackle workshop.

A few minutes later the police withdrew with red-faced apologies. It seemed that Herr Daimler was only a crazy inventor, and was merely tinkering with some sort of new engine, too small to be used as anything more than a toy.

The automobile had been a long-cherished dream since misty

medieval times, but it took the establishment of the industrial age to bring personal transportation, in the shape of the internal combustion engine and a small road carriage, to make the dream a tangible fact.

Gottlieb Daimler, a small-town lad from Bavaria, had worked for some years on stationary engines driven by town-gas, and by 1883 had developed a high-speed engine fuelled by gasoline which was small enough and had sufficient power to be fitted into a crude motorcycle, then into a light carriage. With his designer Wilhelm Maybach he tested his shaky vehicle early in 1886, just a few weeks later than Karl Benz, another German engineer, who was working on similar lines in Mannheim just 60 miles away. Neither knew that the other was developing the world's first automobiles, and ironically, though their companies later amalgamated as Daimler-Benz, the two 'fathers of the automobile' never met.

Daimler's first cars were more in the nature of testbeds for his engines, which he envisaged as power for numerous purposes.

Right: In 1885 Daimler built his first vehicle, a crude form of motorcycle seen here in his original workshop.
Left: A Benz Sociable of 1895, still capable of a turn of speed.

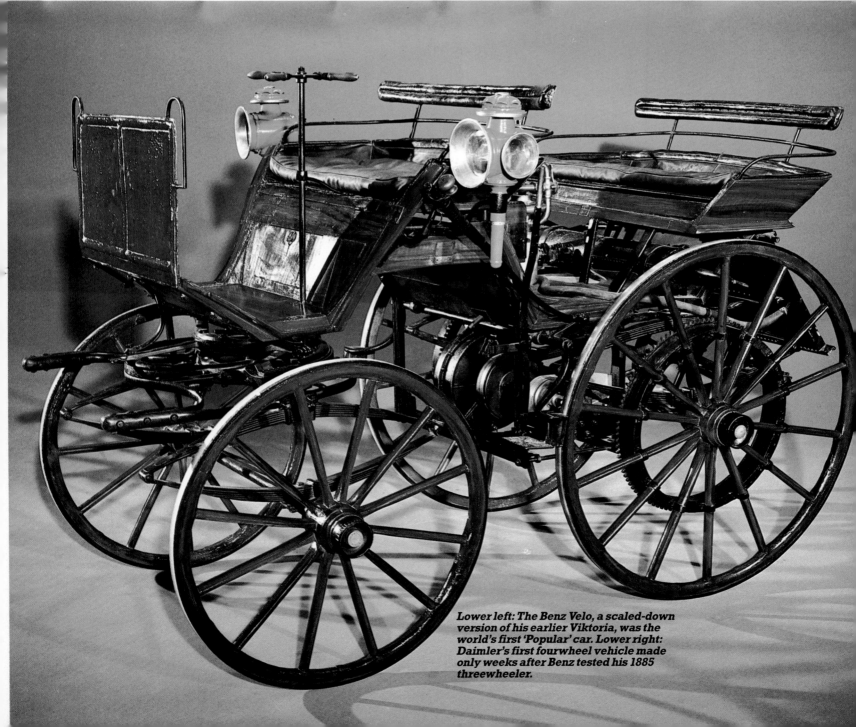

Lower left: The Benz Velo, a scaled-down version of his earlier Viktoria, was the world's first 'Popular' car. Lower right: Daimler's first fourwheel vehicle made only weeks after Benz tested his 1885 threewheeler.

He installed one in an airship, another in a railcar, a riverboat, a fire-engine — but continued making experimental cars. Nobody in Germany was particularly interested, but some of Daimler's engines were built under license in France, eventually passing the automotive lead to that country.

Commercial production of Daimler cars got under way around 1895 and by 1899 the front-engined Phoenix was seen. The car was developed into the first-ever Mercedes, launched to the consternation of every other motor manufacturer in 1901. Compared with the new Mercedes all other automotive products looked like farm buggies; the new car's 35 hp 5.9 liter engine was more efficient, the gear-shift system was new, the pressed-steel frame was an advance, the suspension was streets ahead, the cooling system was revolutionary. Modern motoring had commenced.

By 1911 Mercedes cars had achieved world renown, were bought by the world's rich — and were copied by the world's other automobile makers. A large range of touring and sports vehicles had been offered, building a reputation for racing success and for quality engineering, and the car had grown to a top model of over 9 liters, 90 hp, a speed of 90 mph and called, predictably, the Mercedes 90.

The 1908 French Grand Prix fell to a Mercedes, and the last GP of prewar days, the 1914 French event, was won by a brand new racing Mercedes of 4.5 liters and 115 hp. A few months later this advanced engine was to be found in the fighter planes of the German Luftwaffe.

After World War I, the company started production of supercharged vehicles, first a 40 hp and a 65 hp at the Berlin Show in 1921. Meanwhile 47-year-old Ferdinand Porsche, a designer with a wealth of past experience, had joined Daimler. By 1926 the companies of Daimler and Benz merged. The new Daimler-Benz AG began production of the conventional, reliable Stuttgart and Mannheim models, and the later Nurburg with an 8 cylinder 4.6 liter engine.

Slotted in between these worthies was the magic of the K range of sports cars. First was the supercharged K, in 1926 the

Below: A Cannstatt Daimler 1899, the forerunner of the Mercedes of 1901, a speedster of its day with a capability of 50 mph from its 5.5 liters. Lower right: A 1902 Mercedes tourer, similar in engineering to the legendary original, and right, a 1904 example.

fastest touring car in the world, and from this was developed a great line of sports models: the S in 1927, the 200 hp SS, the SSK, and in 1931 the blown 7.1 liters 6 cylinder SSKL, which won the classic Italian Mille Miglia on its first time out. The designs of these sports world-beaters were the result of the influence of the engineering wizard Dr Porsche, who continued to produce the world's fastest racing cars for the company in the 1930s, the most mind-boggling of which was undoubtedly the incredible 646 horsepower W125 of 1937. The most elegant road car of the period was, it almost goes without saying, a Mercedes, the Porsche-influenced straight-eight 500K of 1934.

In 1947 the prewar models were revived, which after the extremely heavy bombing surprised the industry. By 1954 Mercedes-Benz were back in motor racing, with a team of 'Silver Arrows', the fuel-injected 2.5 liter W196 Grand Prix cars developed partly from the 3 liter 300SL 'Gull Wing' sports coupé of 1952. They had the disconcerting habit of taking the winner's flag in 1st and 2nd positions. Two years in major sport was sufficient for the company to stamp its supremacy on racing and the Mercedes team withdrew, to overt sighs of relief from the rest of the motor-racing world.

In 1964 the Mercedes-Benz range was topped by the 600, an 8 cylinder 250 hp limousine built in the long-wheelbase tradition of the prewar *Grosser* Mercedes, the 'head-of-state' car in which Hitler would take the salute (on a seat raised 5 inches to disguise his lack of height) during parades.

A new generation of 15 different models was seen in 1968, styled on lines that would pass muster today, with high-torque engines for flexibility and three-box safety bodies, a re-design that coincided with the company's 2 millionth car since the end of the war.

Lower left: Mercedes flagship of 1911, the potent 90 had a 9-plus liter engine developing 90 bhp and a sporting speed of 90 mph. Left and far left: The Mercedes 90's powerpack and wheel. Below: The famous 1914 115 hp Grand Prix car that took German driver Lautenschlager to victory in the French Grand Prix of that year.

The 3-rotor mid-engined C111 was something of a mystery. This research-and-development vehicle, built purely for bodywork stress investigation, was later revamped to take a 4-rotor unit and had a number of other refinements that hinted at a future production model. It was, ironically, at 350 hp, far too powerful for road use, and was never developed commercially. The 350SL sports coupé was introduced in 1971 housing a 3½ liter V8 and this highly efficient engine was used in a number of other Mercedes-Benz cars.

Year after year new ranges, new advances, new engines appeared from Stuttgart, and the superbly designed products forecast the current range, which, fined down a little in size and number, includes gasoline or diesel-fueled vehicles from 2 liter up to 5 liters, from the Geländewagen cross-country 44 to the luxury SEC and down to the small-for-a-Merc but still built in the same long-life tradition, the 190.

See the pyramids from a Mercedes — a 1920 poster from Stuttgart. Below: The 1914 Grand Prix car seen recently in action. Right: the Mannheim 370, a touring Mercedes-Benz of 1933. Lower right: The supercharged 6.8 liter Mercedes-Benz S introduced in 1927. Lower left: One of the successors of the 'S', the dramatic SSK: 7.1 blown liters of power.

It's the 190E (the E is fuel-injected; the 190 carburettor fed) that has perhaps captured the public's imagination more than most cars in this category. Using a 122 bhp fuel injected 2 liter with five-speed overdrive setup, it is the smallest Mercedes-Benz to be offered for some years. Its 122 hp takes it up to an all-out speed of 112, way above the legal limit in most countries, although not in Germany itself, where one may often see senior citizens ambling down the *autobahn* at 100 mph.

Treated kindly the 190E yields around 35 miles to the gallon, and has the feel and look of its distinguished marque, although slimmer-built than others of the range. Designed to slot into an executive gap in the market (the only real competitor is the BMW

3-series), the 190 is a beautifully built product that is very much in the 1980s mood, and in the tradition of the company that started the whole business of personal road transport.

Left: Veteran racing driver Hermann Lang demonstrates the 1937 W125. Above: The great Juan Fangio takes the 2.5 liter Grand Prix Merc through a tight corner in 1955. Top left: A 1938 Mercedes-Benz 320 cabriolet. Top right: Mercedes-Benz 300SLR of 1955 Mille Miglia fame.

Top left and above: The 3 liter 300SL, Sports car version of the 300SLR that took British driver Stirling Moss to a sensational win in the 1955 Mille Miglia, the classic Italian race. Far left: The 190SL, a scaled down version of the 300SL; this is a 1956 example. Left: A 1969 250CE coupé, with a six cylinder 150 bhp fuel-injection engine. Overleaf: The Mercedes-Benz 600 the 'state' car designed for the world's elite and large enough to seat a presidential entourage. With 230 bhp from an eight cylinder motor it offered maximum comfort and security.

Top left: A Mercedes-Benz on vacation — a 280S of the late seventies, six cylinder 2746 cc displacement giving a healthy 160 bhp. Lower left: A 1972 300SLC, a development of the earlier 'gullwing' but with conventional doors. Above: The SL theme again — a 450SLC (4.5 liters). Left: The latest product from the Mercedes stable — the 190.

Far left: Hardtop version of the 1974 280SL — 2.8 litres from six cylinders, with fuel injection. Below: The 200D, the four-cylinder diesel first seen in 1969. Left: The Mercedes-Benz 190, launched in 1982.

Above: Third-generation S class, the SEC coupé of the early eighties offered a 3.8 or 5 liter unit. Far right: Backbone of standard Mercedes production, now offered in sizes from 2 liters to 5. Right: The 380SEC fixed head coupé of 1983.

An Earthbound Bubble 1953-1962

Some were no more than a motorized chair on wheels, some were as cramped as parrot-cages, others just a good unworkable idea, yet in the 1950s they were seen on the roads in their thousands, swarming like thirty-miles-an-hour wasps over relatively deserted European byways.

The lightweight 'bubble car craze' began around 1953, although there had been a number on offer almost immediately after World War II in the hope of cashing in on gasoline-coupon rationing. They were hardly family transportation, yet they were better than a motorbike-and-sidecar, and as yet the world had not been introduced to the Volkswagen Beetle or the British Mini.

One of the first of these diminutive bubble cars to ply the roads of Europe was the Messerschmitt — wingless now and powered by a midget 175 cc 2-cycle Sachs engine. Some 10,000 sold in 1953, the first year of production, so popular was its price and so modest its thirst.

Fritz Fend of Rosenheim had originally designed the tiny vehicle as an invalid carriage but when Messerschmitt, the

one-time military aircraft firm, took over, the fighter-plane type cockpit was enlarged to take two people (the rear-seated passenger placed his legs either side of the driver like a two-man bobsleigh team, although how the girlfriend coped was not in the instructions) and a 200 cc unit slotted into the machine. The lightweight KR (Kabinenroller, or Scooter-car) soon became a common sight.

Both the 200 cc, and the Messerschmitt 'Tiger' with a 500 cc motor, were capable of traveling almost indecently fast. Narrow, low and sleek, there was little trouble with wind resistance, and both had an economical performance. The Messerschmitt looked odd, raised a laugh or two — but was, with a dozen other 'bubble'

marques of the fifties, in many ways ideal for those 'austerity' days in Europe just after a devastating war. However, by around 1962 the bubble burst.

The Messerschmitt 'Tiger' was originally designed as a motored invalid carriage, but after the one-time aircraft firm took over it became the 'wingless wonder' — a fast-travelling minicar for courageous couples.

NAG

Germany's First Production V8

Although in 1919 Germany's future looked grim, the former electrical company of AEG had become interested in automotive production, bought a small carmaker, AAG, and had opened for business as Neue Automobil-Gesellschaft, Berlin, or NAG. By 1920 companies were desperately forming survival groups and NAG joined with Brennabor of Brandenburg and Hansa-Lloyd to form GDA, hopefully to rationalize costs and output — and hopefully to stabilize their constantly changing names!

NAG actually profited by this move, despite inheriting a chief designer, Joseph Vollmer, from AAG who was the perpetrator of the Orient Express, one of the most unsuccessful cars of its time with an array of enough hand controls to defeat an octopus. His more conventional automobiles, however, attracted the patronage of the Kaiser's wife and she was loyal to the marque for some years.

The post-World War I GDA grouping policy helped NAG as dominant partner, the Berlin company generating publicity by racing a light, tuned sports version of the standard 2.5 liter 33 hp which scored a convincing win at a Grand Prix held at Italy's newly-opened Monza circuit.

NAG flourished, and bought Protos, makers of the victor of the 1908 New York-to-Paris race. The brilliantly designed (by Paul Henze, leading light of the time) NAG 212 luxury V8, Germany's first V8 to make production status, and a genuinely outstanding car, was shown in 1931. Then a fatal mistake was made, the V8 unit was used with front wheel drive. The result spelled disaster for NAG and by 1934 the company was no more.

NAG purchase. The Presto company of Chemnitz was a good buy for the NAG group in 1927, producing worthy six cylinder automobiles at popular prices. This tourer of 1924 was the basic design for later models.

NSU

The World's First Rotary

The first NSU automobile was born in 1906, although the Neckarsulm company (hence the initials) was already well established, like so many others to take up automotive work, in the motorcycle and bicycle market. Small cars dominated in the first years, and after World War I the firm notched up some significant sports successes with a 1½ liter supercharged car. However in 1930 NSU decided to move back to two wheels, making some highly successful and sportive motorcycles. Later an absolute world speed record for motorcycles was recorded on an NSU machine.

By 1958 a new small car was offered, the Prinz. Made for the new small-car market it housed just two air-cooled cylinders of 598 cc giving a humble 20 hp. It shouldn't be written off as just another buzzbox, however, as it offered a feature that most other makers were not yet bold enough to market — all-round independent suspension.

The firm broke new and dangerous ground in 1963 with the German-designed NSU Wankel, the world's first ever rotary-engined automobile, bodied in an attractive sports spyder style. The three-chambered engine, smoother, simpler than the conventional reciprocating unit, was so small it could be hidden in the trunk. For some time there were sealing troubles, and the engine had a heavy gas consumption. The German tax office had no hesitation, however, in classing the 500 cc unit as a 1500 cc motor, so powerful was its output.

NSU went on to produce the Prinz TTS, a 95 mph 70 hp rorty little job that took its drivers to many a rally win and which in sporting trim also made a mark in touring car racing, and was affectionately dubbed 'the poor man's Porsche'.

The Ro80, launched in 1968, was the company's great pioneering flagship. With its sweeping aerodynamic lines, its silky one-liter two-rotor Wankel engine giving almost 115 hp it was — and still is — one of the most brilliantly designed cars in the story of the automobile, as bold as the breakthrough engineering of the Citroen DS19 of some 12 years earlier. It found a healthy market — some 12,000 sold in the first 18 months — and continued to sell to a selective public for a solid ten years.

During that time NSU had come under the Volkswagen Group control and a second rotary appeared as the VW K70. Japan, permitted to build rotaries under license since 1963, now takes the rotary power unit into the market under the Mazda emblem.

Below: Early rotary, 1965. The NSU Wankel Spyder, a 500 cc mini with the punch of a 1500 cc unit. Right: The pioneering two-rotor Ro80 introduced in 1968 and way ahead of its time.

OPEL

The House that Adam Built

Sewing machine manufacturer Adam Opel's five sons were dedicated cycling fans; with others who had discovered a new mobility at the end of the nineteenth century they pedaled energetically through the German countryside on their precarious high-wheelers. Opel senior noted the trend, took advice from British cyclemakers, and started to produce a 'safety' cycle at his factory near Frankfurt.

Carl-Jörns, Wilhelm, Heinrich, Fritz and Ludwig, however, were products of their time and could see that the gasoline-driven horseless carriage was already rumbling over the horizon. By 1898 they had bought the rights of a machine designed by an engineer from Dessau and the first Opel-Lutzmann was completed, a one cylinder 5 hp machine that could struggle up to around 12 mph.

A Paris visit brought back a contract with the French Darracq firm to import chassis to which the factory fitted bodies.

Top right: The first Opel to be made completely at the Russelsheim works was this 1902 twin-cylinder 12 hp tonneau. Center left: Opel's first horseless carriage, the Opel-Lutzmann of 1899.

Lower left: By the time this 1909 double phaeton was produced Opel was firmly established. Below: The 1912 5/14 hp tourer affectionately known as the 'Puppchen' (Dolly) for its dainty looks.

Meanwhile the Opels designed and built the first of their own models, a 10/12 hp with a front engine. The Opel brothers quickly brought out new and better models, first a two-cylinder car, then in 1903 a four-cylinder model. By now Opel were firmly established in the automotive field, consolidated by the success of Fritz and Carl-Jörns' Opel in motor racing, a sport which had recently become important for its publicity value.

During this first decade of the twentieth century Opel was the unchallenged leader of the German motor industry and by 1912 new modern production techniques enabled them to celebrate their 10,000th car manufactured.

Opel continued to expand into commercial vehicles and during the years leading up to World War I popularized the torpedo shape — a soft-top design showing a clean straight line in profile along the top of the hood and doors. Motor sport was not neglected and as early as 1913 an Opel produced record and race vehicles which developed up to 110 hp — and one of 260 hp. In 1918 French occupying forces broke up the Opel plant and for a few years the company had to maintain their racing activities in prewar cars. However, the Opel firm, still in the hands of the family, learnt fast, mainly from visits to the United States. By 1924 Opel had installed a conveyor belt system.

World demand changed, necessitating fewer models and higher production. Opel's immediate answer was the 1924 Laubfrosch, a little 951 cc 12 hp 'Tree-frog', so called because of its reptilian green color. It became Germany's most popular car. Meanwhile Opel's experiments with rocket-propeled cars took them into a field that was to be further developed in wartime.

Opel's phoenix-like recovery, mainly due to the Laubfrosch, captured 31 per cent of Germany's car exports and 25 per cent of home sales and by 1928 Opel had its best-ever year, rivaling American designs and quality, although Opel's inventive talents produced some models that bore a strong US stamp. The German automotive industry had, however, a limited market and the first shadows of the great depression could be seen. The Opel family formed a joint stock company in 1929, with General Motors of Detroit (who already had a local assembly plant) taking a large share, and becoming sole owner by 1931.

Below: The Opel 6/16 hp Torpedo, the last vehicle to be made at the Opel plant before a devastating fire destroyed the factory. It was developed into the popular Puppchen. Lower right: Another version of the 1912 Puppchen, this one is a two-seater with rumble seat. Right: Opel's best seller of the twenties, the 12 hp four-cylinder Laubfrosch (Tree-frog).

The next decade saw Opel producing three model ranges, the first appearing in 1931 when most of the other German motor companies were grinding to a standstill in the financial winter of the time. And just before US runner Jesse Owens was collecting his gold medals at the Berlin Olympics in 1936, Opel launched their 1.5 liter all-steel Olympia, the 500,000th car to emerge from their works. That same year saw the new Kadett (a model whose production plant finally ended up in the Soviet Union, becoming the Moskvich) and by 1938 the 6 cylinder Admiral was the company flagship.

After World War II the Olympia and the Kapitan rolled off the lines again within three years of occupied peace, little changed in looks from the prewar products, and a new Kadett was seen. A significant step was taken when the 5.4 liter Chevrolet V8-engined Diplomat was introduced in 1965.

The Commodore GS appeared in 1970, a high-performance six with optional fuel injection, and a year later the public saw the new Manta, Opel's answer to the Ford Capri. Since then the too-prolific range of models of the 1970s (which included a Kadett which later became the foundation for an entire new generation of GM small cars to be made around the world) has been fined down and today's top car is the Opel Monza GSE 3.0E, a 3 liter fuel-injected straight-six with an available 180 bhp. Its maximum of 132 mph may be a little over the top, but its 5-speed gearing means that 70 mph is maintained at a sleepy 2,700 rpm. The car typifies the startling GM improvements that have been made, particularly in Germany and Britain during the past decade.

Left above: Opel's 1938 flagship, the six-cylinder Admiral. Lower left: The Kadett range introduced in 1974 proved ideal for family and sports work. With its 993 or 1190 cc unit it quickly became a high seller. Above: Based on the CD, an experimental seen at the 1969 Frankfurt Show, this Opel by Frua has a drag-coefficient of just 0.4. Below left: An Irmscher Manta 240.

Current Opel Kadetts in various sizes and tune are mirror-image of the British GM product the Astra, all of which have capabilities of over 100 mph. Here a range of Kadett GSi versions show their lines and paces.

PORSCHE

Amazing Pace

On 12 October 1984 Niki Lauda became World Champion driver for the third time, with team-mate Frenchman Alain Prost runner-up. Both were driving McLaren Grand Prix cars, which were awarded the Formula 1 constructors' championship for the year — just one of the many major achievements of Porsche of Stuttgart in the last 30 years. Specifications had broadly been set for the power plant by both the McLaren team and the French consultants of TAG, but the essential V6 design and construction were Porsche.

Significantly, Ferdinand Porsche had always been competition-conscious. In earlier days he had designed and developed the power plant for the famous pre-war Auto Union Grand Prix racer, he introduced torsion bar suspension, and an 'unbeatable' synchromesh gearbox which was pure joy to use. There is virtually no field of serious motor sport which has not at some time been dominated by Porsche, from Le Mans to Daytona, Targa Florio to Grand Prix racing.

The company has played so many tunes with their race-bred models by switching around engines and chassis that it is impossible to list the profusion of identi-numbers other than as an index. Porsche's practise has been to introduce a more powerful new engine and make it available in a well-tried chassis. Then, when further engine development puts the power up, they design and introduce a new chassis, etc.

The most famous racing Porsche must be the 917. Ferry (son of Ferdinand) Porsche gave the green light for this creation in June 1968 when the World Manufacturers' Championship was open to prototypes up to 3 liters or sports racers up to 5 liters. The 917 was on show in Geneva only eight months later. By May 1969 the required minimum of 25 new models had been built and sold, and ten days later the 917 raced at Spa in Belgium. The model helped to take three world titles, winning 15 events, including two at Le Mans, and the Daytona 24-Hours. Under 5 liters, with a horizontally opposed, air-cooled unit of 12 cylinders with four overhead camshafts the car had a maximum power output of 620 bhp!

For the public at large the consistent favorite was the 911. Unveiled in 1963 as a 2 liter producing 130 bhp, by 1978 it could extract 300 bhp from a 3.3 liter turbo power unit, a truly astonishing climb. Both on road and track the engine went on growing — from 2 to 2.4 to 2.7 to 3 to 3.3 liter. Most popular in the late 1970s was the 911 SC with its flat-6 air-cooled 3 liter giving a punchy 180 bhp.

Below left: Early Porsche. This 1100 cc Type 356 was produced in 1952 but the model has been seen on the road for three years by this date. Right: A Porsche 356 Roadster corners at speed during a recent 'historic car' race. Below: The Spyder RS60 of 1960 at speed in competition.

In addition to the years of success with the 911, a major eye-catcher in the Fall of 1984 was a 911 Group B design study. This is a potential contender for the coming world championships in racing and rallying, with four-wheel drive and a daunting 400 bhp.

It surprises some experienced drivers that such high performance sports and sports-racing cars have been, and still are, offered with automatic gears. But the Sportomatic transmission, like so many Porsche features, is unusual in that the car can be driven almost like an automatic but the gears can also be changed at will as with a normal manual box.

In the present Porsche range, which includes the timeless 911 in different versions including turbo, interest centers on the 924, 944 and the V8-engined 928S Series 2 automatic. The 924 is a sports car built to a (relatively) low-cost budget, while the 928 is built with perfection rather than cost in mind. The 924 sprang from an original commission by Volkswagen and became a Porsche as we know it when the latter took over the NSU plant near Stuttgart. But not all the VW links could be broken. The 2 liter engine is basically a VW-improved version of the Audi 100. Porsche brotught the power up to 125 bhp — good enough for a low-drag body and low fuel consumption. Almost the full circle, as the first Porsche engines to be put in the early 356s of the fifties Volkswagen-based units.

Below: Porsches with special high-revving engines used in competition were labeled Carreras, after the Mexican Carrera Panamericana race; this one is the Abarth version. Right: Since the 911 was launched in 1963 it has been firmly established in its several forms as the classic road Porsche. Bottom: The transient 'Volkswagen-Porsche' 914 of the early seventies Overleaf: Also in the classic mould, the Porsche 911 2.7 liter Carrera shows its pace. Inset: A 1973 2.7 liter 210 bhp Carrera RS.

Right: The Martini Team's potent 917, a 4½ liter flat-12 with startling power at 520 bhp. Above Right: The 1974 Porsche 911 Carrera RSR Turbo. Below: The 917/30 Spyder.

Far left: This long-nosed 935 of 1978, a water-cooled twin-turbo at 750 bhp, was in effect a 911 at its most extreme shape. It won a number of top-grade events during its career. Called 'Moby Dick' by some as it looked a little like a whale ... Left: A 1982 Porsche 956 of the Rothman Racing Team; a great endurance car that won several world titles. Below: Porsche's 928S, today's top-of-the-line in front-engined design, introduced in 1978 with 4½ liters and 240 bhp.

RUMPLER

The Teardrop Car 1921-1926

It has a nostalgic charm now, with its upright profile and lateral aerodynamic lines, but in 1921 the new Rumpler Tropfenwagen (Teardrop car) sent a ripple through the automotive design world that provoked some fundamental changes. Aerodynamics was a word not yet in the dictionary and its principles had been tried (at speeds where it counts) by only one or two fearless auto engineers.

Dr Edmund Rumpler was in effect a struck-off aero-engineer — as were all such German engineers immediately after World War I when they were forbidden to work on aircraft design. He turned naturally to automobile design.

Rumpler's first work had been for the Frankfurt company Adler back in 1904 when he created Germany's first engine to be built in unit with its gearbox, although he had been a young apprentice fetching and carrying for the Bohemian Nesselsdorf company when they made their first Benz-based car in 1897. His talent, he

thought, lay more in aeronautics, and in 1907 he joined the infant industry, later designing the bat-winged Traube monoplane used in the 1914-18 war.

Back with earthbound designs, Rumpler's airflow experience led him to work to aircraft principles, and the Tropfenwagen, sensation of the 1921 Berlin Show, showed it strongly. The rear-mounted six cylinder 2.6 liter engine was again in unit with gearbox and final drive, and the engine was totally new in concept with three banks of two cylinders, alloy pistons and overhead valves.

The driver sat centrally right up front with all-round vision, the passengers in the usual place, and the teardrop bodyshape was the classic aerodynamic form, a light steel hull with flat fin-like fenders, curved windscreen and single headlamp — as much airplane as automobile.

Its maximum of 70 mph, due mostly to its streamline shape, caught the interest of Benz, and Rumpler was asked to make a Grand Prix car. Benz staff made the cigar-shaped body and Rumpler the chassis. The Tropfenrennwagen (Teardrop racer) got 80 hp and 100 mph from its 2 liter Benz engine, and at its racing début it clocked 4th place. Not bad for a first timer, and its racing future seemed bright. But once again economic factors struck down a promising project and little more was heard of the car.

Plenty more was heard of Rumpler though — he designed another Teardrop, although an unsophisticated public at large was not ready for this sort of innovation, so it was modified to a more conventional pattern. By 1926, continued national financial chaos sadly wiped out his projects and his little company, but there is still much in modern design that can be traced back to the strange engineering talents of Edmund Rumpler, born about 40 years too early.

Former aero-designer Edmund Rumpler showed this astonishing vehicle at the 1921 Berlin Motor Show. Its six cylinder 2580 cc engine was set in arrowhead formation in three banks of two — a completely new configuration.

VOLKSWAGEN

One of the 8,987 Volkswagens produced in 1947, with rear-mounted air-cooled 1131 cc power unit. Today's VW Beetles, still made in Brazil and Mexico, look much the same although housing more sophisticated and larger engines.

Small Wonder

The idea germinated in the mind of Ferdinand Porsche, born in what is now Czechoslovakia, former technical director of Austro-Daimler. From his youth he had been interested in small cars and in 1930 he opened a design office under his own name in Stuttgart. It was here that he made the first drawings of a small cheap car, and it was here that he did the preliminary drawings for a remarkable 'Porsche' 16-cyl engine which ultimately powered the famous Auto Union racing car.

In 1934 came the demand from the German government for a design for a real 'People's Car'. Dr Porsche's prototype, made in his garage at home, had the characteristic flat-four aircooled engine at the back; with a 985 cc capacity it developed a modest 23.5 bhp at 3000 rpm. During 1937 there were 30 more prototypes running in a punishing test program, built by Daimler-Benz and in Porsche's new workshops at Stuttgart.

The final production version appeared in 1938 (the VW38) with 704 or 984 cc engines, and in the same year construction began on the new factory with the car then being called the KdF-Wagen. The people, of course, did not get their car, for it was destined in various forms for military use in World War II.

In 1945 two-thirds of the VW plant at the so-called town of KdF-Stadt (now Wolfsburg) was in ruins. It was right at the eastern edge of the British zone and what tiny output the factory had maintained went mostly to the British Army. Just 1,785 VW Beetles were made that year.

The Allies discussed the future of the Volkswagen plant. The British took a Beetle home, looked down their noses, and said no thanks. The Ford spokesman from the USA said 'Not worth a damn!' and the Russians said 'We wouldn't mind it if you would kindly move the border back a little.' So it stayed where it was.

A major turning point came in 1948 when ex-Opel executive Heinz Nordhoff was appointed to run VW. His dynamic example helped 7000 VW workers to cut the time of around 300 hours per car to 100, and that was done while they worked standing in pools

Right: The wartime Kommandatur, basically a Beetle with winter tires and military fittings. Its air-cooled unit proved impervious to desert heat and Russian cold but it could not compete with the American Jeep for mobility. Below: Standard Beetle, clothed by Hebmuller.

including McPherson strut at the front. On 17 February 1972 Beetle broke the Ford Model T record when it passed the 15,007,033 production figure.

The Beetle was discontinued at the Wolfsburg plant in 1979. European demand was now for more sophisticated vehicles, but the People's Car, transformed over the years in mechanical specifications though not much in shape, had sold more than 19 million.

VW had in 1969 introduced the unitary construction 411 followed by deviants which now bring much commercial success, such as the K70 derived from the Ro80 following acquisition of the

of water up to their ankles, with rain dripping through the roof, and with 'shaky legs and empty stomachs' as one worker said. Nordhoff himself spent six months living in the factory, sleeping at night on a camp bed. By 1949 he had proved his worth with a range of standard and deluxe model Beetles and the cabriolet — an open version of the deluxe introduced by Karmann.

Through the next years a program of improvements continued; but the range of three main models remained the Standard Beetle, deluxe version and the Cabriolet. For the US market there were a few extra changes, mainly confined to different bumpers for greater protection against four-wheeled US hardwear. By 1967 the range was 1300 cc, 1500, and a new 1500 cc cabriolet. 1971 saw the 1.6 liter 'Super Beetle' with extensive suspension changes,

Audi-NSU combine. The water-cooled front wheel driven Audi 80-based VW Passat appeared in 1973 with 1.3 or 1.5 liter engines, beam rear axles and servo-brakes, from which the logical development was the stylish Scirocco, followed by the best-selling Golf/Rabbit. It had a transverse-mounted engine originally of 1093 cc, but today it has five engine sizes, giving from 45 to 112 bhp, and includes a convertible. In 31 months one million examples had been sold, and it remains the current VW best-seller.

The Polo arrived in 1975 to fill the growing market for the three-door hatchback market and there is now a larger sedan and a coupé version, and the Jetta was introduced to extend the market for the Golf/Rabbit by having a four-door sedan body. The latest model is the Santana, flagship of the fleet with a choice of engines up to the 115 bhp fuel-injected 2 liter.

Although Europe may have grown out of it, Ferdinand's Porsche's little Beetle, the People's Car that brought modest transportation to so many millions all over the world, is still alive and well — and rolling off the assembly lines in Brazil and Mexico.

Top left: The amphibious VW Schwimmwagen. Some 70,000 waterborne Beetles were built during World War II. Center: The classic VW Beetle of the mid-seventies. Now offered with a 1300 cc unit but few styling changes — the definitive shape hardly changed during its long production run — the little car had become the most popular seller in Europe, and has a large following in the United States. Bottom right: VW by Bilter. Edrich Bilter's design firm was used by several specialist builders in the 1960's and '70's.

WANDERER

Germany's Little Doll

A large number of light cars offered during the lean years of the early twenties were dangerous wire-and-bobbin concoctions with qualities somewhere between an automobile and a sewing machine. The early Wanderer was one of the more solid exceptions. Although when it first appeared in 1911, it could be mistaken for a flimsy with its two-seater tandem layout (one occupant seated behind the other), its 4 cylinder 1150 cc shaft-drive engine and its quality materials put it in the true small-car class. The Puppchen (Little Dolly) as it was known, was in fact Wanderer's first factory-designed venture into the four-wheeled field, although whilst it was on the drawing board the company had turned down a very similar blueprint from a young engineer named Ettore Bugatti. Ettore eventually sold his project to Peugeot of France who called it the Bébé, now of immortal fame.

The Puppchen grew up, losing its name, acquiring a 1220 cc 15 hp unit and another seat at the back, leaving the driver in a solitary central front position. Used during World War I as communication vehicles, the little car was made until 1922, by which time Wanderer Werke offered the model with power units of up to 2 liters.

The thirties saw more impressive Wanderers. Six-cylinder examples had been built since 1929 and now the car was available in 3 liter sports form. The 2 liter W25K (mit Kompressor) appeared in 1936, from the drawing board of the energetic Dr Porsche (who seems to have designed every car in Germany) who had joined the company. The truth was that he had actually designed the car for Daimler-Benz who had not taken it up, and had since sold it to both Steyr of Austria, and to Wanderer. However, it was a Porsche vehicle in the best tradition with a top speed of 93 mph, but was made only in small numbers until 1939. The company had joined the life-preserver group Auto Union in 1932 but although the names of some of its companies were brought back into the market after the war, the line that began with the Little Doll was seen wandering no more.

A Mercedes-Benz 220 coupé of 1960. The fuel injection 220 was introduced in 1959.

Back endpaper: One of the fastest and most luxurious racing cars in the world, the Porsche 934 a derivant of the 911.

PICTURE CREDITS